A GUIDE TO Up the Ladder: Acces
Grades 3–6 Writing Units of Study

MW01614417

Lucy Calkins

Photography by Peter Cunningham

Illustrations by Marjorie Martinelli

HEINEMANN ◆ PORTSMOUTH, NH

The Up the Ladder series is dedicated to the heroic teachers who have gone to the ends of the earth to invent their own versions of this series, out of an effort to provide all kids with access to a state of the art writing curriculum.

Heinemann
361 Hanover Street
Portsmouth, NH 03801–3912
www.heinemann.com

Offices and agents throughout the world

© 2017 by Lucy Calkins

All rights reserved. No part of this book may be reproduced in any form or by any electronic or mechanical means, including information storage and retrieval systems, without permission in writing from the publisher, except by a reviewer, who may quote brief passages in a review, with the exception of reproducible pages, which are identified by the *A Guide to Up the Ladder: Accessing Grades 3–6 Writing Units of Study* copyright line and can be photocopied for classroom use only.

The author has dedicated a great deal of time and effort to writing the content of this book, and her written expression is protected by copyright law. We respectfully ask that you do not adapt, reuse, or copy anything on third-party (whether for-profit or not-for-profit) lesson-sharing websites. As always, we're happy to answer any questions you may have.

—Heinemann Publishers

"Dedicated to Teachers" is a trademark of Greenwood Publishing Group, Inc.

Cataloging-in-Publication data is on file with the Library of Congress.

ISBN-13: 978-0-325-09657-5

Editor: Tracy Wells
Production: Elizabeth Valway
Cover and interior designs: Jenny Jensen Greenleaf
Photography: Peter Cunningham
Illustrations: Marjorie Martinelli
Composition: Publishers' Design and Production Services, Inc.
Manufacturing: Steve Bernier

Printed in the United States of America on acid-free paper
21 20 19   VP   3 4 5

Contents

Acknowledgments

THE UP THE LADDER SERIES stands on the shoulders of decades of prior work, and all of the co-authors join me in thanking those who've helped us develop those big shoulders. We're grateful to 'the Dons'—Don Graves and Don Murray, the two people most credited as co-fathers of the writing process movement. They've both been gone for almost a decade now, but at the inception of their work with writing process, I was their junior colleague, and their torch was long ago passed on to me and to the Teachers College Reading and Writing Project. We carry it with pride.

These units extend, reiterate, and clarify the curriculum that members of the Teachers College Reading and Writing Project community have been working collaboratively on for a very long time, and we're grateful to all the current and former staff developers at the Project. Some Project staff have been particularly influential in developing curriculum in the three genre. We especially thank Mary Ehrenworth for her contributions over the years to the Project's thinking about narrative writing, Annie Taranto and co-author Kelly Boland Hohne for their work with opinion/argument, and Colleen Cruz and Emily Butler Smith for their help with information writing.

Above all, this series carries the DNA of TCRWP staff members who especially champion the urgent need to adapt curriculum in ways that give access to all learners. We especially thank Amanda Hartman, Cornelius Minor, Colleen Cruz, Jennifer DeSutter, Janet Steinberg, and Natalie Louis for their advocacy and urgency. Our former Senior Deputy Director, Kathleen Tolan, was particularly dedicated to the cause of providing access to all kids, and her brilliance as a teacher has informed all that any of us do.

These books are briefer than usual, the language, more spare. Many of the ideas are iterative. We thought, therefore, that they'd be easier to write than the others but working on them, we've been reminded of the writer who once said, "I'm sorry I wrote such a long letter. I didn't have time to write a short one." The twin goals of brevity and clarity are not easy!

The units were as challenging to write as other units have been, and as always, we cannot be more grateful to the team of writers and editors who pitched in to help. Thanks to Julia Mooney and Katie Clements for sometimes putting the load of these units on their backs and carrying it for a bit, allowing co-authors to catch their breath. We were inspired by the way you progressed up a switchback or two, doing so with such grace and delight. Thanks also to Karen Kawaguchi and Tracy Wells, our editors from Heinemann, who have edited the series of units of study books and have our curriculum and methods in their DNA. Thank you for drawing on years of experience to keep our form consistent, our choices deliberate.

These books are comprised not only of words but also of images and videos. The TCRWP has a team of artists, and each of these people gave generously of their time and talent. We thank Marjorie Martinelli, Kimberly Fox, and Elizabeth Franco. What joyous, intuitive art, and what a difference the art makes in the job of giving all kids access. More people contributed by videotaping themselves giving minilessons, and we thank those who did and Tim Lopez for the actual work of filming almost 60 minilessons.

People who do not write for publication sometimes think that books are made at the writer's desk, but in fact, it truly does "take a village" to make a book. For TCRWP books, it takes *two* villages—one at Teachers College, Columbia University and the other in Portsmouth, New Hampshire. There are a few geniuses at Heinemann who have had a hand in the entire Units of Study line, and that list is topped with Elizabeth Valway. Elizabeth leads the design team, which is no small endeavor. The layout of the units makes them infinitely more potent, and deciding where to insert which piece of student work and which coaching text falls on Elizabeth's shoulders. Lisa Bingen leads the effort to bring these books to you, our readers, and she couldn't bring more enthusiasm, passion, and energy to that mission. Abby Heim directs all things TCRWP, and is one of my closest friends. She can scold me, coach me, rally me, and she does this for the entire writing team. I couldn't imagine pulling this off without her.

For decades, Peter Cunningham's photographic artistry has internalized the dimensions and the messages of the Units of Study, and he drew on that knowledge to bring children into the pages of these books.

I want to thank all the teachers who piloted the Up the Ladder units, and especially the teachers of Danbury, Connecticut. Three of Danbury's elementary schools had received staff development for years from the Teachers College Reading and Writing Project, while the other schools in the districts had been left to fend for themselves, teaching a district curriculum without TC staff development. This fall, all the principals formed a study group, and came to realize that it was time for everyone to come aboard the Units of Study curriculum. The schools that had never received staff development needed an infusion of energy, and a leg-up: the perfect context for the Up the Ladder books.

Teachers throughout five Danbury schools agreed to pilot the Up the Ladder units—and you'll see the results, in abundance, in the student work and the photographs that fill the pages of these books. Suffice to say that the co-authors and I could not be more touched by the extraordinary progress those children made, and we salute the children, their teachers, and the entire city of Danbury.

Above all, I thank the co-authors who joined me in making this series a reality. Kelly Boland Hohne, our anchor person on all-things-argument, brought a fierce determination to make the opinion book perfect. Celena Larkey's knowledge of the foundations of opinion writing, her verve and her ability to kid-test everything breathes special life into that book. Mike Ochs is famous for his generosity of time, thought, and talent, and he lived up to that reputation once again with this series. Alicia Luick has a legendary work ethic and she brought that, plus endless grace, to the mission. Hareem Atif Khan has ghost-written parts of TCRWP books from her home in Pakistan, and now, as a full-time colleague, drew on her remarkable talent as a writer and her delight in learning to more than rise to the occasion of co-authoring the information book. She was my constant ready companion, always. Methods of staff development are in Shana Frazin's DNA, and she reminded us to always think about the teachers who are learning to teach through these units as well as the students learning to write. This team of co-authors could only do our work because of other co-authors that have gone before us, and whose ideas informed our work, and we thank all of them—Christine Holley, Mary Ehrenworth, Colleen Cruz, Valerie Geschwind, Marjorie Martinelli, Amanda Hartman, and others, too.

Welcome

Dear Reader,

Welcome, come in. How I wish I could lead you to a chair close to a crackling fire, and pull a seat alongside you, settling down to hear about the journey that has led you to be here, on the first page of this book. As much as I love the written word, I'd much rather be the person to help you across the threshold of this series.

Above all, my colleagues and I want you to know that these books embody the one mission that is closest to the hearts of all of us at the Teachers College Reading and Writing Project. For us, the most important word in the title of these books is this one: *access*.

Nothing matters more than the mission of giving all young people access to the beautiful, important work that happens in reading and writing workshops.

Giving access to the richest possible writing instruction—and through that, to the power and beauty, awareness, and intimacy that comes in a writing workshop—isn't just a hum-de-hum, run-of-the-mill aspiration. It is one of the cardinal principles of our profession. It's the mission of our lives.

We've written the Up the Ladder units to give you and your children access to what we believe is the richest and most research-based writing curriculum on earth: the Units of Study.

To help you understand what I mean by giving your students access to the Units of Study, I need to give you a bit of background on some of the behind-the-scenes decisions made during the development of the writing units. When we worked on the Units of Study, we had to make a choice whether to "make shoes that fit—or shoes to grow into." We chose the latter, writing that curriculum for kids who are growing up within Units of Study

writing workshops. This means that each Unit of Study assumes students have experienced the unit that came before it. But that, of course, won't be the case for upper-grade students entering writing workshop for the first time. The problem is that when students in grades 3–6 enter a writing workshop without those years of experience, they can be overwhelmed by units on argument and research-based information writing and the like. This will be especially true if those writers' literacy skills are not strong in the first place, or if the writers are learning English as a new language, but it is also true for writers who may find it easy to produce well-spelled neat pages but who haven't been taught to hone their focus, to elaborate on their ideas, to write with voice. As soon as my colleagues and I realized that we had inadvertently invited some kids onto a ladder whose lower rungs had been sawed off, we knew that we needed to give those kids a leg up.

These Up the Ladder books are designed to help classes filled with upper-grade students who are currently working below benchmark levels in writing or who are new to writing workshop instruction. The units are designed to meet students where they are and to accelerate the development of their skills in narrative, information, and opinion writing. The research and beliefs that underlie Universal Design for Learning influenced us as we created these units, selected strategies and materials, and thought about ways to give all students access. The Up the Ladder units are designed to be absolutely engaging for students in grades 3–6, but our primary goal has been to ensure that students make dramatic progress.

Best wishes,
Lucy

Chapter 1

An Overview of the Up the Ladder Series

THE RELATIONSHIP BETWEEN THE UP THE LADDER BOOKS AND UNITS OF STUDY

The Up the Ladder units are designed to be precursors to the Units of Study themselves. The three books that constitute the Up the Ladder series were written to be taught in sequence—first Narrative, then Information, then Opinion—and are written in ascending challenge level. The Narrative unit is the easiest; the Opinion, the most challenging. The books align to each other, and there are many aspects of one that are echoed in the others. Each unit should last no more than five weeks at the very most. Although written to be taught in sequence, the three units can each also work when taught out of sequence.

There are many ways that a teacher can slot the Up the Ladder units alongside the four units in your grade-level kit of Units of Study in Opinion, Information, and Narrative Writing. You might choose to:

- Alternate between Narrative Up the Ladder and a grade-specific narrative unit, then do the same for Information and for Opinion.

- Use one of the Up the Ladder units to start your year, and then proceed through your grade-specific Units of Study kit until you encounter an upcoming unit that feels especially challenging. When that happens, use the aligned Up the Ladder unit to provide your students with a ramp to that unit.

- Start your year with the three Up the Ladder books, then proceed to the four Units of Study books.

Some people ask whether it is possible for the three Up the Ladder books to be distributed across the grade levels so that, for example, the Narrative book gives a leg up to third-graders, the Information book to fourth-graders, the Opinion book to fifth-graders. The answer to that question is yes. Teaching in sequence (first Narrative, then Information, then Opinion) will have advantages, because the later books in the series make some references to the earlier ones. However, we encourage you to experiment with all the possible ways in which these resources can be useful to you and your students.

The Up the Ladder units follow the same format and are informed by the same principles as the Units of Study. Because the Up the Ladder books have been written several years after we wrote that initial series, they reflect what we have learned from helping teachers teach the first series.

A significant difference between the Up the Ladder books and the original Units of Study is that the sessions in the Up the Ladder series are much shorter and simpler than those in the original series. Also, each minilesson comes with a QR code that links to a video where you can watch a Teachers College Reading and Writing Project staff developer teach that minilesson to the camera. These videoed minilessons are far from perfect—first, because there are no students present, and second, because we prepared for them as we imagine you'll prepare for a minilesson, giving ourselves just ten or fifteen minutes to read the session and to make a few charts. Although these are far from ideal, we hope they help you pace your teaching of these minilessons so they last less than ten minutes.

Those of you who are familiar with the Units of Study will recognize that the checklists, mentor texts, and tools those units offer to help kids self-assess are present in this Up the Ladder series as well, but in a simplified form. That is, we have adapted the checklists from the Units of Study and given students a similar but shortened version. Our hope is that these more abbreviated checklists still contain the essentials of the longer checklists, and yet are even more accessible than the checklists contained in *Writing Pathways*.

You won't want the Up the Ladder units to take the place of the original Units of Study. That curriculum has been taught in thousands of schools and has led to extraordinary results. Those results aren't a surprise—the team that wrote the Units of Study in Opinion, Information, and Narrative Writing has been fortunate enough to learn, throughout several decades of collaborative practice, from the most brilliant and dedicated teachers imaginable. We've also been able to draw on the wisdom of the scores of experts from across the world, that TCRWP brings to New York each year. That is, each and every unit bears the fingerprints of many brilliant teachers of writing. The units are also aligned to ambitious world-class standards. The series has been influenced by many contemporary calls, including calls for teacher effectiveness assessments, Depth of Knowledge, digital literacies, performance assessments, teaching for transfer, collaborative learning, Universal Design for Learning, Next Generation Science Standards, argument, and critical literacy. So yes, we think the Units of Study in Opinion, Information, and Narrative Writing are uniquely special.

We are aware, however, that when teachers first encounter Units of Study in Opinion, Information, and Narrative Writing, the challenge of coming to know those units, to differentiate essential from nonessential, can be overwhelming. We know the units especially ask a lot of any teacher who does not receive TCRWP professional development. The good news is that we've written the Up the Ladder units to give *you*, as well as your kids, access to Units of Study in Opinion, Information, and Narrative Writing.

Up the Ladder: Narrative Writing Checklist

Beginning		I brought my reader into the world of the story. I may have done this by: • Showing who was in the story • Describing where the story was taking place • Including small actions that were happening
Middle		I showed what the main character did. (The main character is me in a personal narrative.)
		I helped readers picture what happened. I did that by telling it bit by bit and by telling what I (or the character) did and said and thought.
Ending		I tried to make a good ending. I might have put a final action or feeling or lesson at the end.

But for now, let's turn our focus to the nitty-gritty details of the series, and to the adventure that awaits you.

THE THINKING THAT INFORMS THE SERIES: HOW DO WE GIVE WRITERS ACCESS?

There are three units in the Up the Ladder series, and each contains twenty to twenty-two sessions. These books have been designed for children in grades 3–6 who may not yet have had many opportunities to practice writing narrative, information, and opinion/argument pieces, or might not have had those experiences in workshop-style classrooms. The units aim to support students in writing with increasing volume and with growing skill and sophistication.

The TCRWP staff spent a long time studying how to successfully accelerate children's growth in each genre. We analyzed the progression of skills taught in each kind of writing across the elementary and middle school grades and worked analytically to locate key skills within those learning progressions and standards. For each of the three genres, we devised a pathway supporting the development of especially key skills. The units are designed to give young people the opportunity to engage in repeated successful practice and to move along a gradually increasing progression of challenges.

A Short Time Frame for Intense Writing Practice

In the first portion of each of the three units, youngsters write one text after another, starting and finishing the draft of a text within a single writing workshop. In the Narrative unit, for example, kids write *three* personal narrative booklets within Bend I (Week One). Each time they write a story, they first touch the pages of their three- to five-page booklet, telling aloud the story they will write, then they quickly sketch the story across those pages, and finally they write a small paragraph (or a few sentences) on each page, completing the story in a day.

Meanwhile, in the Opinion unit, students begin by bringing collections of things they cherish to school—ticket stubs, baseball hats, friendship bands—and they nominate one item as the best in the collection, and write a nomination, announcing and supporting their judgment. They write several nominations a day, learning they can nominate one item as best, another as worst. They anticipate different opinions, responding to those counterarguments with more reasons and with evidence.

Whereas upper-grade writers in the Units of Study books work for a week or two on a single piece of writing, the Up the Ladder units begin by asking students to start and finish texts within a day, returning to those texts the next day to revise them.

The short time frame means that youngsters never lose sight of what—or for whom—they are writing. They shift quickly from planning to drafting to revising, internalizing the writing process. The fact that youngsters plan for piece of writing they'll create that same day makes that planning especially potent, and the fact that their writing will be revised tomorrow helps them draft the texts quickly (as flash-drafts).

Revision is especially attractive because it is concrete and manipulative, with youngsters cutting their drafts apart and either inserting swatches of paper or stapling new versions of portions of their draft on top of the first version.

Strategies from Primary Grades that Promote Universal Access

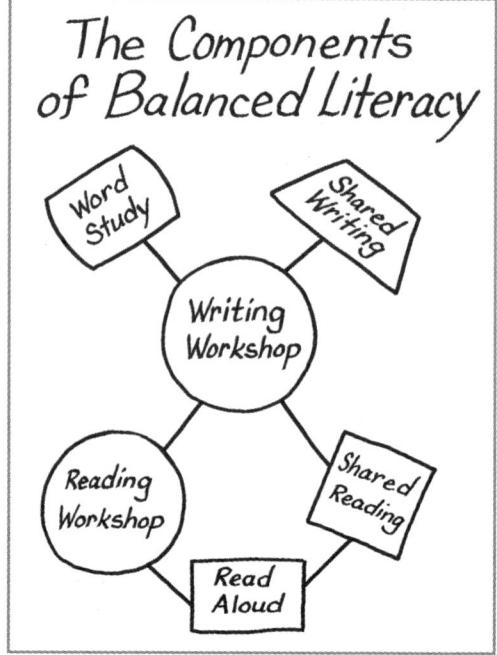

Teachers who know Units of Study in Opinion, Information, and Narrative Writing well will see that some of the strategies featured in these new units have been imported from the primary-grade-level Units of Study. For example, in the first-grade unit on information books, children learn that to plan out the sequence of subtopics to address in a chapter, it helps to sketch those subtopics down the margins of their pages prior to writing. That strategy reappears in the Up the Ladder books, although it's reincarnated differently; it is embedded in the content, topics, and mentor texts that are appropriate for grades 3–6. Bear in mind that the Up the Ladder books are meant for novice writers—older students, but still beginning writers. So it makes sense that these books adapt tools and strategies that have proven over decades to be especially potent for novice writers in primary classrooms.

You may wonder about the wisdom of incorporating strategies from lower grades. Years ago, Jerome Bruner pointed out that the essence of any subject can be taught to anyone at any age. In the teaching of writing, this is certainly true. A seven-year-old can reread his or her draft, choosing the most important part of it to expand, stretching out the heart of that draft. That work is appropriate for the seven-year-old. A PhD graduate student can do that same work, and the work would be appropriate for that scholar, too.

This idea is at the heart of the concept of access. Universal design is about making things more accessible, not "easier." So, a lever doorknob is useful to people of different abilities and needs—to someone with arthritis, to a person carrying something and using an elbow, and to the person with full use of her hands. Using primary strategies to teach writing doesn't make it "easier" or "babyish," but rather creates something that all students can benefit from, no matter where on the progression of development they might stand.

A writing task can be equally challenging and interesting for a seven-year-old and for an adult. Who among us wouldn't find it challenging and thrilling to attempt to write a series of easy-reader fiction books, reminiscent of the Henry and Mudge or Poppleton books, with each book featuring the same characters encountering new predicaments? In the primary-grade unit *From Scenes to Series: Fiction Writing* from the Units of Study, first-graders are invited to try this challenging work. Meanwhile last semester, fifteen graduate students and staff developers attempted the same work within the context of a writing course taught at Teachers College by the renowned writer, Sarah Weeks. Mike Ochs, one of the coauthors of *Up the Ladder: Accessing Narrative Units of Study*, was a member of that course, and he brought his experiences to the Up the Ladder narrative book where again, children are invited to write their own series of fiction stories, akin to those in the *Poppleton* series.

The fact that writers of varied ages can all find this work challenging is not surprising. Bruner is right that the essentials of any subject and certainly of writing instruction are relevant for any learner at any point. The truth is that all of us want opportunities to engage in work that is demanding yet attainable, and the work these units rally youngsters around is always just that.

Promoting Students' Accountability to Themselves

By the time students are in the upper grades, it is not enough to teach them the essentials of strong narrative, information, and opinion writing. They need to be held particularly accountable to producing work that reflects what they are being taught. So, throughout these units, you'll see many times when kids are asked to pull out the writing they have been working on and to double-check it. "Put a C beside the claim in your review," the kids are told in the Opinion unit, for example. "Put R1 beside your first reason, R2 beside your second. Make sure you have examples to support each reason."

Then, too, kids are often asked to lay out the first book they wrote at the start of the unit, and to look at this alongside their latest text. Is their writing dramatically better now than it was when they wrote that first book? If not, get to work this instant! In the series, students are taught to review and revise their writing using charts and checklists that highlight genre-specific qualities of good writing. When writing nonfiction books, for example, students lay their drafts alongside a checklist that asks them to assess whether their text's beginning gets readers ready to learn about the topic. Has the writer tried to make the beginning special, perhaps by asking the reader a question, by painting a picture with words, or by telling a story on an interesting fact? Youngsters read that checklist, then examine and revise the beginnings of their information books to double-check that they have implemented the instruction.

The tips in this series aren't presented just as fun options. There is a clarity and a firmness to the instruction, and everything that is taught is followed through on. Although the Up the Ladder units are written to be especially motivational, they are also authoritative and even a bit bossy.

Providing Opportunities for Rapid and Dramatic Growth in Writing Complexity

The other thing you will notice is that these units progress at a rapid pace. Your students will see themselves growing before their eyes. This growth will be dramatic, in part because their work at the start of the unit will not be especially high level. When we piloted the units, the first sessions caused some raised eyebrows. "Isn't this going backward?" some of the teachers worried. "Really? This paper seems almost babyish," some fretted. Because this was a pilot and we were experimenting, we asked the pilot teachers to trust in the plan, to teach it with heart and soul, pretending (for now) that they were convinced of the wisdom in it, and we promised to alter things if that was their recommendation afterward. However, within a few days the teachers reported back saying, "Oh my gosh, this is *so, so* right. The volume and the energy! It is unbelievable. You'd have to see it to believe it."

Because students begin each unit by producing quick flash-drafts of writing, making texts that they can whip out within a day, and because students receive lots of repeated opportunities to create small,

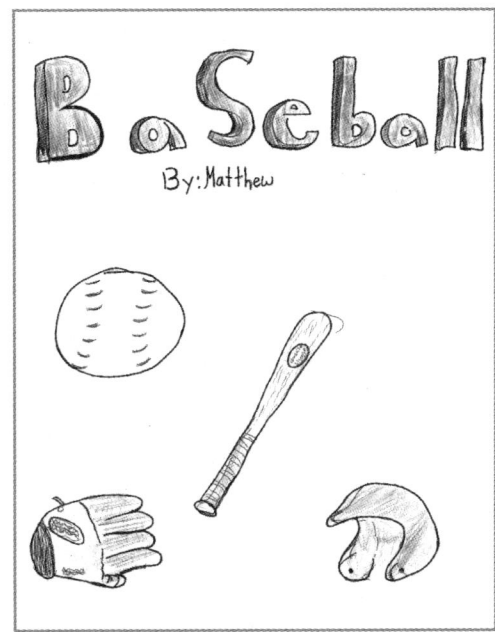

Matthew gets the reader ready to learn about his topic by asking a question.

successful bits of writing, students quickly internalize the most essential characteristics of the kind of writing you are teaching. For example, because children start the Opinion unit by writing lots of nominations in the first bend of the unit, they quickly internalize the structure of writing with a claim and supportive reasons, so this becomes second nature to them.

Children no sooner grasp the most basic elements of the kind of writing you are teaching than they are asked to tackle more complex writing challenges. The child who has nominated one of her friendship bracelets as the best in the Opinion unit (and argued why a different bracelet is her worst) now progresses to writing reviews in which she continues to put forward an opinion and support it with reasons and examples. Again, she will write several reviews—of restaurants, movies, video games. She studies mentor texts of reviews, noting the way authors hook their readers by talking directly to them, for example. Once writers have spent a week writing reviews, the unit asks them to tackle yet a third kind of opinion writing—persuasive speeches. Now students argue for changes to the school—and once more the demands escalate and the significance of the work deepens.

In the Narrative and Information units, too, kids progress equally quickly so that their work grows in length and complexity before their eyes. Kids are told, a few days into these units, "Put the first book you wrote in front of you, and put today's writing beside it. Is today's writing *way* better? Check to see that you wrote more on each page. Count the details in your first piece, count the details in today's writing. Your writing needs to be getting way, way better. If you didn't add more details, quick! Do so now." In the Narrative unit, kids move from writing simple narratives from their own lives to creating a series of fictional stories. By the time they reach the final bend, students graduate to notebooks and to work that constitutes a "writerly life." Each of these stories is built from several small-moment vignettes. In the first, what the characters do and say shows trouble beginning . . . and by the story's end, another small-moment vignette shows the trouble being resolved.

From the start to the finish of a unit, students' engagement with the writing process deepens. For example, at the start of the Information unit, writers revise in concrete ways—anticipating the questions that readers will ask (*who? what? where? why?*) and then answering those questions at the bottom of the page. Soon, writers learn to chunk their information into paragraphs. This leads them to create paragraphs that are sometimes small and underdeveloped, so writers are taught techniques for adding new information into each appropriate paragraph. This revision work may involve cutting a page apart to add in space for an example. It may involve adding a flap over one introduction and rewriting that introduction on the flap. By the third bend, writers take one of the books they wrote in a single day at the start of the unit, and spend an entire week revising that book, turning a little three-page booklet into either a chapter book or an article with subheadings. Now their revision includes doing research to gain more concrete information, adding that information into their chapters, and studying writerly craft in mentor texts, then emulating that craft in their own writing.

A student develops a narrative story idea.

Contrast this sort of work with the challenges that fifth-graders are asked to do in the Units of Study opinion-writing unit, *The Research-Based Argument Essay*. In that unit, students engage in a multiweek project that involves sustained, large-scale work researching into the pros and cons of whether chocolate milk should be served in schools. Given the complexity of that work, you'll understand how important it is to provide students with access to those upper-grade units of study by starting them off with these Up the Ladder units.

If the work in the Units of Study sounds out of reach for your students, know that you're not alone. But know, too, that in classrooms that have piloted the units, the most important takeaway teachers have shared is that their kids' writing *could* and *did* get better before their eyes. Once students have participated in the Up the Ladder units, they are primed to learn to sustain work across a sequence of weeks, shifting from researching a provocative topic, to citing texts and embedding citations into their drafts, considering counterarguments, and revising their large research through a scission of drafts.

Online Digital Resources

I would be remiss if I did not mention the online resources that accompany the series. These offer you a wealth of resources and tools to support your teaching. You will find charts you can print out, student work samples to use as mentors, checklists for your students to use to self-assess, links to digital texts mentioned in the units, and so on. I encourage you to go to Heinemann.com and register your set of the Up the Ladder units right away so you can access these online resources.

To access and download all the digital resources for Up the Ladder:

1. Go to **www.heinemann.com** and click the link in the upper right corner to log in. (If you do not have an account yet, you will need to create one.)
2. **Enter the following registration code** in the box to register your product: UTL_VYWE8
3. Under **My Online Resources**, click the link for **Up the Ladder**.
4. The digital resources are available under the headings; click a file name to download.

(You may keep copies of these resources on up to six of your own computers or devices. By downloading the files you acknowledge that they are for your individual or classroom use and that neither the resources nor the product code will be distributed or shared.)

Chapter 2

Methods and Structures for Teaching Writing

T HE WONDERFUL THING ABOUT TEACHING WRITING is that there are only a handful of methods that are used repeatedly across every grade and every unit. The predictability and clarity of workshop instruction makes it easy for you to become something of an expert in workshop instruction. All you need is to grasp the predictable structures of every day's writing workshop, to learn the handful of methods that you will use every day, and then to begin teaching the units. Your teaching—your work with the curriculum—will not only teach the kids, it will teach *you*. The first time you teach a unit, it will take a lot of work to acquaint yourself with the unit and to understand the content that you are teaching. But the next time you teach that unit, it will be worlds easier. Your immersion in the units will help you develop expertise on writing development and curriculum.

THE PREDICTABLE SCHEDULE OF EVERY DAY'S WRITING WORKSHOP

Writing workshop—in fact, any workshop—is deliberately designed to be a simple, predictable environment. You can understand the principles that inform a writing workshop by thinking about a pottery workshop, a painter's studio, a researcher's laboratory, a scholar's library. Each of those environments is deliberately kept simple and predictable because it is the work at hand that is changing and complex.

The predictable structure of each day's writing workshop undergirds the Units of Study. Each session, in all of our units, is a day, and each day's writing workshop is fifty to sixty minutes. Each session begins with a minilesson. Kids sit with a long-term partner while in the minilesson. The minilesson ends with the kids being sent off to their own independent work. As they work, you confer with them and lead small groups. In the Up the Ladder books, as in the Units of Study, a section of each session discusses the all-important teaching you'll do during each day's work time. Halfway through that time, you'll stand and deliver a mid-workshop teaching point, in which you cajole the writers to do something you believe matters. Sometimes that mid-workshop interval channels students to share with their partner. The workshop ends with a share, and often this interval also sets kids up to show their partner the work they did that day.

You will notice that at the start of every session, there is a section titled "In This Session" that begins, "Today you'll . . ." The first part of that blurb crystallizes the focus for that day's minilesson, capturing that day's teaching point. You'll also notice that most teaching points have also been captured and illustrated on large Post-it® notes that accompany each unit. You can use those Post-it notes to construct an anchor chart that cumulates the most important points of your teaching.

The anchor chart in a unit of study is important because on any one day in a workshop the work that kids are doing will not necessarily match that day's teaching point. Instead, students draw upon all they've learned up to and including that day's teaching point, and that culmination of teaching is captured in the anchor chart. The work that students do in a day will also be crystallized in the second part of the opening blurb that comes at the start of every session. It will be important to use this blurb to shape your expectations (and in turn, your students' expectations) for what will be accomplished in a day's work time. That is, more specifically, on the day your minilesson focuses on writing endings, some writers will be starting, not ending, their books, and therefore they'll be apt to draw on instruction from earlier days, instruction that helps them with generating ideas, planning, structuring, and starting a draft.

Of course, some of your students will accomplish more than others in a day's writing workshop. Their progress won't always be totally in sync. However, keep in mind that during the writing workshop, there is no such thing as finishing work early and doing something else. This is writing time, and everyone cycles from one piece of writing to another. This means that if a student decides not to revise his or her book (and you don't reach the student to influence that choice), the alternative to revising one book is to write another one. As a result, some children (often the ones currently needing more support) will write two or three books in the same amount of time that others write and revise one. And of course, some students will write more in one book than others write in two books. It is extremely important for you to keep in mind that the paper used by different students will be different; some includes space for an illustration, some contains giant margins, and some is regular notebook paper (you'll find templates for different paper choices in the online resources).

IN THIS SESSION

TODAY YOU'LL teach students that writers can bring out their characters' quirks by adding the characters' secret thoughts and feelings.

TODAY STUDENTS will be finishing and revising their second fiction story. They will draw on the entire repertoire of revision strategies and all they know about how good fiction stories go, as well as highlight the secret thoughts that bring the quirkiness of their characters to life.

A CLOSER LOOK AT THE ESSENTIAL STRUCTURES OF A WRITING WORKSHOP

Let's slow down and examine the structure of a day's workshop. We'll begin with a brief overview, then explain everything in more detail below.

Overview of a Day's Writing Workshop

Across every grade, every writing workshop teacher begins by convening his or her students for a brief minilesson. Every minilesson follows a predictable architecture, which allows students to anticipate how this time goes.

After the minilesson, students have time to work on their writing. As they work, you'll confer with them and lead small groups. In the Units of Study, the small-group and conferring section within each session conveys the most important ways your writers will need support that day. As students work and you move among them, there will be times when you find yourself wanting to say the same thing to every writer. Those are times to stand in the midst of the room, ask for all students' attention, and give what we refer to as a mid-workshop teaching point.

Finally, each day's writing workshop concludes with a share session, inviting students to remember and reflect on what they learned that day. They'll often get a chance to share their writing and get feedback from partners and will sometimes gather as a class to share insights on how to improve their writing.

This structure for a writing workshop has been around for decades. Each day contains the perfect combination of whole-class, small-group, and one-to-one instruction, and each day provides lots of opportunities for independent practice.

The Minilessons (less than 10 minutes)

The brief minilessons that begin each day in a writing workshop are generally given in the classroom meeting space, with kids sitting in assigned rug spots, each beside a long-term partner. This is a time for teacher-led explicit instruction, so instead of seating students in a circle, teachers usually pull them as close as possible. For a deeper discussion about minilessons, see the "Inside the Minilesson" chapter in *A Guide to the Writing Workshop*.

Structure of Minilessons

While the content of minilessons will change from day to day, the architecture remains largely the same. Minilessons contain four component parts: Connection, Teaching, Active Engagement, and Link.

Paper choice of illustration box with nine lines for text

Paper choice for a "How To" piece of writing

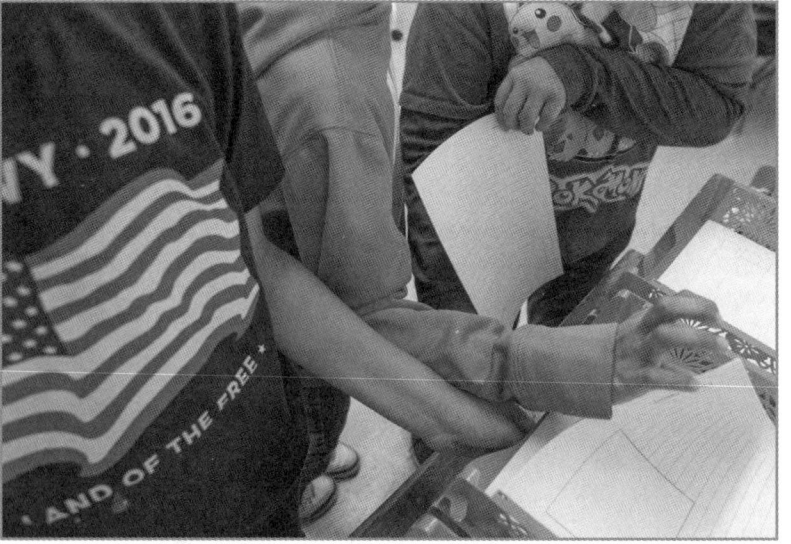

Connection (approximately 1 minute)

Minilessons begin with a two-part connection. The first part *connects* the day's teaching to the ongoing work that children have been doing. You might share tiny excerpts of student work or explain a challenge or success the class has experienced. Sometimes the main job is to recruit kids' interest.

In the second part of the connection, you name the teaching point of the day. An effective teaching point is crystal clear and usually conveys that today's session will help writers do something that they will want to do often as writers, and then teaches them one way to go about doing that. That is, teaching points generally include a goal and a step-by-step strategy.

Teaching (3–5 minutes)

In the teaching portion of the minilesson, you usually demonstrate the step-by-step way in which you go about doing something. Often you work on a piece of writing that threads through many of the minilessons. To solicit youngsters' engagement in the teaching portion of a minilesson, you may convey, "Will you help me as I . . . Let's work together to . . ." Although you invite kids' participation, in the end, you demonstrate, so once you have kids sitting on the edges of their seats, anticipating what you'll do, you pull ahead and demonstrate the strategy you are teaching.

Active Engagement (1–3 minutes)

In the active engagement, students try to do what you demonstrated in the minilesson. Everyone participates—sometimes working with a partner, sometimes on his or her own. Prior to those interludes, you might, for example, suggest, "Give me a thumbs up when you have thought of *one* way you know to revise your information books." Then you'll wait for half a minute, scanning the group, as one kid after another signals with a thumbs up.

Once many children have signaled that they have an idea, you will then say, with great urgency, "Turn and talk!" Once youngsters are accustomed to these turn-and-talk interludes, it takes just seconds for them to shift in and out of these conversations. Sometimes, then, you may call for several turn-and-talks within a single minilesson. The key is to keep these brief, and to refrain from following them with whole-class conversations. You'll sometimes want a brief interlude for one or two students to report back after the partnership conversations—we have found it is often most expeditious for you to recap rather than asking kids to do that. "I heard some of you saying . . . and then again, I heard . . ."

The writing (or, more likely, the writing-in-the-air) that kids do during the active engagement will amount to no more than a few lines in length. Students do not write entire pieces from start to finish within a minilesson. Instead, partners may help each other imagine how they'll describe the way a character walks into the room, or the transitions they use to insert a quote into their draft. Sometimes, this writing adds onto a demonstration text that the teacher has also worked on. Other times, the teacher might bring a problematic text to the minilesson, saying, "You've heard about my neighbor, Otis, who sometimes comes

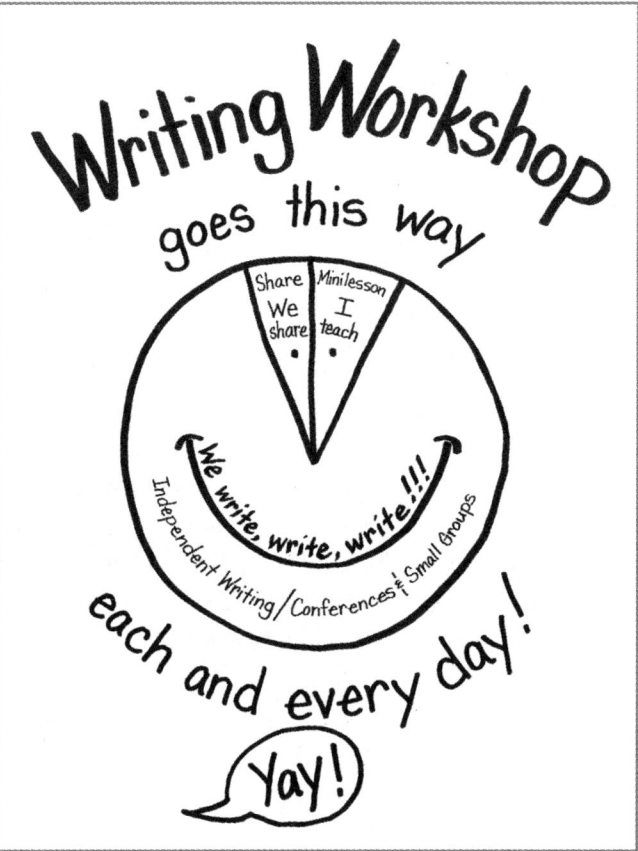

by in the evenings for help with his writing? Last night he brought me this piece. Will you help me think about how to help him?" Always, during minilessons, teachers find ways to get kids involved so that they are not just passively learning, but instead apply what they have learned.

Link (1 minute)

Minilessons end with a link—the term that is used to signal that this is a time when you ask youngsters to transfer all they have learned from whole-class instruction to their ongoing work. Often during these final moments of a minilesson, you attach an enlarged Post-it that captures that day's teaching point onto an anchor chart that threads through the unit. Typically, as children head off to work, you remind them that they can either tackle the new work of the day, or draw on all they have already learned.

Pacing of Minilessons

The minilessons are designed to be brief—no more than ten minutes—to maximize the time your students have to write. Keeping your minilessons brief may sound daunting, but it is actually easily done. To help you see how manageable this is, we have videotaped ourselves giving each minilesson in this series to an imaginary class of kids. The videos are very basic—we're just sitting in front of the computer, transcript in hand. You'll see that we paraphrase some parts and read aloud others, and that we shift between looking at the (imaginary) kids and glimpsing the page of the book in hand. Most teachers we know do this as they teach. Most importantly, these videos will help you get a sense of the pacing that the minilessons require to give your kids the maximum time to write. You'll find QR codes for the videos in each session, and those codes will take you to the videos.

Each minilesson is the result of many cycles of writing, piloting, and revising. Always, a team of co-authors will have spent at least a full day working on each minilesson, and often several days. We will have tried many times to tighten the minilesson so that the teaching is as brief and clear as possible—with the goal that you should not have to do the same. We hope our work allows you to spend more of your time studying your children's work, planning ways to confer and lead small groups so that each of your writers has the access he or she deserves.

Until you are experienced as a writing workshop teacher and have internalized the structure and pace of minilessons, we advise you to trust the minilessons as they've been written—paraphrasing them a bit, swapping your own kids' names and examples in place of other kids' names and examples—but staying close to the plan.

When we piloted these units, we found that teachers had some predictable but solvable problems with pacing, not only within the minilessons themselves, but also across units. If you find yourself running over time, you may find that you are encountering one of these predictable problems:

- **Expecting immediate mastery.** Minilessons are meant as rallying cries, as keynotes. When taught well, they pump up the energy and create a sense of common cause in the community. But no one masters a writing skill by hearing about it! Mastery of any skill, including writing, takes time and repeated practice. Bear in mind that almost any concept you teach in one unit will be taught several times in that unit, and again in the next unit, and again next year, and on it goes. These Up the Ladder units, as well as the Units of Study, will give your students repeated opportunities to practice their skills again and again, so that over *time* they can master these.

- **Overtalking.** If you are unsure that every child has grasped your teaching, and you find yourself repeating and discussing each portion of the minilesson, asking kids questions, inviting their input, and hearing possible draft ideas from the class, you are overtalking. Overtalking has serious consequences. The kids get bored, the instruction gets muddy, and above all, there isn't time enough for kids to write. When there isn't time enough to write, students' work gets significantly out of sync with the minilessons and problems multiply.

- **Extending minilessons over more than one day.** Sometimes, in an effort to scaffold kids or to support mastery, teachers break sessions apart, teaching a single session across a whole sequence of days. Teachers are especially apt to do that when a minilesson teaches a big concept—say, revision—and includes a few examples of ways to do that bigger thing. In those sessions especially, teachers sometimes take each example, each subordinate item, and teach it separately. That spotlights the expendable instead of highlighting the main point. It weakens the momentum of the unit and makes the unit take much longer to complete than it should. Keep in mind that the units have been designed to be taught within four to five weeks (and you could teach them in a considerably shorter time frame, since this time frame includes a few "catch-your-breath days").

- **Adding more minilessons.** You may be tempted to add related minilessons to a unit, but we recommend that you do so only sparingly, as too much added content can turn a coherent, trim unit into a hodgepodge. The pace of each unit as designed supports coherence, creates an aura of urgency and intensity, and allows you to teach a sequence of seven units across the year.

Later, in the chapter "Addressing Predictable Concerns," I'll discuss some of the other challenges that surely crop up during minilessons. For example, we already know that there will be times when you call on a child during a minilesson and he produces some whack-a-doodle response—something that isn't close to the answer that the minilesson led you to expect. We know, too, that there will be times when you teach a minilesson and you are left unsure that kids "got it." What to do?

Work Time (Students should have 35–45 minutes to write each day while you confer and lead small groups.)

The most important words of the minilesson are the final ones. "Off you go," you'll say, and your students disperse to their work spots, open their writing folders, and figure out what their work will be. Then they write—and this writing time is the part of the workshop that you and your students will cherish the most.

A student works to add dialogue to her story.

Go to great lengths to protect this time. This means ensuring that writing is taught every day, just like math and reading, and it means limiting the length of your minilessons to no more than ten minutes. It also means teaching kids to self-manage, to carry on with independence, so that you are freed from constant management and able to respond to students' writing.

As your students work, you can expect they will draw on a repertoire of strategies, developed across the days of your unit (and across other units, too). That is, they will not just be doing what you taught them to do that day—they will be working on their writing, using all they have learned to do. Not all of your writers will be in sync with each other, but this is as it should be. Think of a pottery studio. Some students will be ready to make their lids before others, but all of them will progress along as potters, doing the work their pots call for them to do.

Support Engagement

The most important way to manage a writing workshop is to make the work highly engaging. We know this is true, instinctively, but neuroscience backs us up on this as well. Practitioners of both differentiated instruction and universal design for learning agree that for a student to learn, first that learner must be engaged. This is especially true if there are obstacles (inexperience, a learning difference, or an emotional concern) that might make learning more challenging. If you imagine bringing fabulous colored marker pens and lovely sketch pads to your class and inviting kids to draw alongside or before they write, chances are that some of the management challenges you run into will take care of themselves, because a fair portion of the class will be able to sustain work with engagement. Your goal when teaching writing is to make the writing work itself equally engaging. I'm not suggesting it is as easy to get your kids as engaged in writing as they'd be in drawing, but thousands of teachers throughout the world will tell you that the beautiful, surprising thing about a writing workshop is that yes, indeed, many kids do start loving to write.

There are lots of ways these units support that engagement. First and foremost, the kids are writing on topics and for audiences they care about. They are making stuff—books, speeches. They are watching themselves get dramatically better, seeing their work pay off in visible growth. People are responding appreciatively to their writing and their ideas. They are being treated with enormous dignity, as if they are professional authors. Their quirky, personal brands are being appreciated. Writing time allows them to move about: to gather on the floor, to disperse to work areas, to talk often with peers. They have choices of paper, and it is fancy looking. They have a variety of cool pens in different colors. All of that will go a long way toward helping you keep your class on task, working with fervor.

If you find that kids nevertheless have a hard time sustaining their focus on writing, then you'll probably want to use the mid-workshop teaching as a time for partners to read what they have written so far to each other, and to say aloud what they plan to write next. You'll do no harm by adding an interval for talk that meanwhile gives kids the satisfaction of reaching an audience and also an opportunity to rehearse. Some teachers find that it helps to have two mid-workshop teaching points, one that tends to be a voiceover ("I'm hearing some of you turn the page. Good job reaching the end of one page and turning to the next. You all should be close to the bottom of the page by now") and the other, an interval for sharing.

There are management tricks that can help. For example, we find that if you leave a writer who feels stuck at his or her table for any significant length of time, that youngster is apt to distract everyone else at that table. Some teachers find the best solution is to say, "If you are totally stuck and need help, come to me." Then, that writer can follow you as you confer with other children. This keeps the youngster under your influence, and meanwhile can often result in some nice learning. The writer who is stuck will benefit from the opportunity to eavesdrop on your instruction to other kids, and chances are you can at some point say, "Did that tip help you as well?" and then send the writer back to work. In any case, you will have kept the youngster from pulling others off task.

You'll want to teach youngsters that if you are in the midst of another conference, they can pull close and listen in, but they absolutely cannot interrupt you. If they do, look astonished. "Couldn't you see I was having a . . ." and your tone needs to turn almost holy, ". . . *a conference? Is it an emergency? Because otherwise, you don't interrupt a conference!*"

Finally, if you find some of your kids are having trouble being engaged in writing, think about whether there are some alternate ways to give those kids access to writing. For example, you might invite a few youngsters to use voice-recognition software so that they can still maintain writing independence while dictating their writing, or else to use a laptop or tablet with software that anticipates words the student is trying to write, or has translation capabilities. Many students who currently seem stymied by writing production find that using writing technology that supports independence, while simultaneously removing or reducing composition obstacles, can allow them to find their voices and use their latent writing skills. The important thing about this technology is that it produces a written draft, and that draft can be revised.

Supporting Volume: Paper Choice Conveys Expectations

The volume of your kids' writing matters tremendously. Writing well has a lot to do with writing fluently. Only when writing fluently does the lilt of oral language come through on the page, and only then can the writer elaborate on a thought and follow a line of language. This means that just as you need to be sure your kids are not word-by-word readers, you also need to be sure they are not word-by-word writers. If you see a youngster write just a couple of words, then pause, then return to the page to write another word or two, intervene. "Actually, the way you write is you have a thought—a whole thought. Then you write, write, write without stopping until you get that whole thought onto the page. Usually that's where you put a period. Then you have the next thought—another whole thought—and you write, write, write 'til it's on the page."

The Up the Ladder units are designed to boost your students' writing volume. In both the Narrative and Information Up the Ladder units, writers are expected to write whole books on the first day of the unit. In the Narrative unit, this is a personal narrative story, while in the Information unit it is an all-about book on a topic the kids know well, but in both books, every child is expected to write that whole piece in a day. In either case, students may write a skeletal text, but your confidence can convey to them that they can complete the whole book in one day—no problem. And it is true they *can* all do this, so long as they realize from the start that the job is to write an entire story or an entire book *in one day*.

How can novice writers write an entire book in one day? It all has to do with something as mundane as paper choice. In the online resources, you'll find a number of templates you can use for writers at different levels and for different types of writing. For beginning writers, you might make booklets from paper that has only a few lines for writing and a large space for sketching. As students become more proficient, you'll channel them to booklets in which the paper contains more and more lines, and smaller sketching spaces.

We have found that writers (especially struggling/resistant ones) are more successful when they are given paper that they can successfully fill. If a particular kind of paper requires a quantity of writing far beyond what a child can produce, that writer will give up hope of filling the page. Instead, he'll just eke out a few lines on the top of the page, and leave most of the page empty. But if that same child writes on paper that he can (with some resolve) fill, the page itself acts as a goal post, rallying the writer to write more.

One of the biggest surprises we encountered when working with the pilot classrooms was the realization that the paper put before children conveys powerful expectations for their writing in ways that can hold a writer down or can spur a writer forward. As soon as a writer comes close to filling the pages on which she is writing, you must be vigilant enough to notice and to say, "You are ready to graduate. Let me move you to this next kind of paper." Always, the page itself should beckon the writer on. Alter the paper on which kids write so that it is always just a step ahead of their current level of work. If a youngster easily filled a three-page booklet, with each page containing five or six lines, make sure that the next time she sits down to write, her booklet is five pages, not three, and each page has twice the number of lines for writing and less space for sketching. And if that child fills up only a tiny portion of a page, act surprised. "What happened here? Is your plan to go back and write more on each page?"

You can expect this series will make a magical difference in the volume of writing your kids do—so long as you firmly believe this is possible. If you enter these units certain that most of your kids can't possibly write three-page booklets in a day, then they won't. If you are uncomfortable asking kids to sustain work on their writing, then they won't. Your expectations become your kids' ceiling.

16

Providing a Clear Model

Just as your expectations for volume matter, your expectations for the sort of text your kids are writing also matter. This is why we include samples of student writing in the Up the Ladder books themselves and in the online resources. Study the student work, noticing ways in which you see evidence of the instruction coming through the texts. Your students may enter the unit at higher or lower proficiency levels than the writers whose work is included, but either way, you should be able to learn from a close study of the work.

You will see that several times in each of the Up the Ladder units, we have provided a simple, bare-bones example of the sort of text your students should be aiming to write. You'll use the texts to demonstrate key strategies that you want your students to learn. In Narrative, you'll demonstrate in Bend II with a story about a girl named Lizzie Harper who wants a dirt bike, while in Bend III you'll use a narrative about a cat named Snuffie, who ran away during a family outing. In the Information unit you'll work with an all-about book on fireworks in Bend I, in Bend II you'll demonstrate with a class book on "Kid Injuries," and in Bend III, you'll revisit "Fireworks." Similarly, in Opinion, you'll demonstrate with reviews of "The Stew Pot" and "Yummy Pizza Kitchen" in Bend II, and move to a persuasive speech, "We need to Recycle Better" in Bend III.

In addition to your own demonstration writing, each Up the Ladder unit channels you to use mentor texts with your students. Published authors regularly immerse themselves in the work of others, and studying mentor texts with your students allows them to have this same experience. Mentor texts provide students with clear direction, helping them develop a vision for what strong writing in that specific genre looks like. As the poet Lucille Clifton once said, "We cannot create what we cannot imagine."

In Narrative, you'll invite students to study *Shortcut* by Donald Crews and *Poppleton* by Cynthia Rylant. These mentor texts will give students a vision of the genre they are aiming to write, and allow them to investigate moves authors make. Then, in the Opinion unit, students will study awards, reviews, and other kinds of persuasive writing, asking, "Is this writer doing something I can do in *my* writing?"

Of course, you will also want to invite students to study mentor texts on their own. That way, when students have a question, they can turn to a mentor text for a possible answer instead of raising their hands to ask you. For instance, a student who wonders, "How can I add details to my writing?" could pull out an excerpt from *A Seed Is Sleepy* and study how Dianna Hutts Aston added details. Then, she could return to her information book and try adding details in that same way. What an empowering experience for a young writer!

You can expect that when you first ask, "What did this author do that you could try?" your students will say, "Oh, Cynthia Rylant told that Poppleton used to do lots of city things like taking taxis and jogging and going to museums." You'll want to coach kids to think less about the content of mentor texts and more about the craft moves the writer has made. You might say, "Cynthia Rylant wrote that Poppleton used to do lots of city things, but that wouldn't make sense in your book, would it? You wouldn't start talking about the city things your character used to do! Let's see if we can name what Cynthia Rylant did so you can

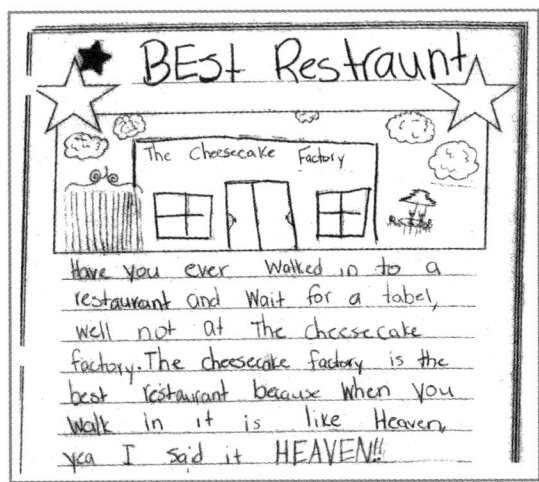

Kari's review of the Cheesecake Factory

consider trying to do something similar in your own writing." As students experience the Up the Ladder units, expect to see their skills at studying mentor texts improve.

Cycling through the Writing Process

During any writing workshop, when working with writers of any age, it is easy to answer the question: What are the kids doing? Writers are writing. Of course, writing involves a whole array of component activities, and writers shift between those as their project demands. One way to talk about this shifting focus is to say that writers spend time rehearsing, drafting, revising, and editing. Those are the four terms that Pulitzer Prize–winning writer, Donald M. Murray, selected to describe the process that every writer, working on every project, is apt to go through. For a deeper discussion about the writing process, see the "Upper–Elementary-Grade Writers and the Writing Process" chapter in *A Guide to the Writing Workshop*.

Rehearsing. Whether a writer is a poet, a speech writer, or an author of an Up the Ladder unit, he or she will rehearse for writing. Most rehearsal takes place away from the desk, as one talks, observes, teaches, thinks, reads, researches, plans, imagines toward the prospect of an upcoming writing project. As the time to put hands on the keyboard, or pen to paper, draws closer, rehearsal changes a bit. Writers map out possible structures. For example, to plan the sequence of a narrative text, writers sketch the content of each of their pages, chunking the story they aim to depict into scenes (or small-moment episodes) that become the beginning, middle, and end of the story. Information writers find that making table of contents can be a way to divide a topic into subtopics. By thinking about the sequence of those chapters, writers explore different ways to organize their treatment of the topic.

Perhaps the most powerful way to rehearse for writing is to say the text aloud before writing it. When the text is a narrative, writers sometimes tap the pages of a book, storytelling a new part of the story with each tap. When the text is informational, oral rehearsal often involves writers teaching others.

Drafting. Rehearsal gives way to drafting. At the Teachers College Reading and Writing Project, we often use the term *flash-drafting* to represent the way we think drafting works best. "Write fast and furious," we say. "Throw down the words. You can come back later to fuss with them." Of course, there is no *one* way of drafting that works well for every writer, but for most youngsters, it works best if they write drafts quickly, focusing on their subject. Writers who write drafts quickly are more apt to revise, and revision is essential—both for the eight-year-old writer and for the professional writer.

Revising. Re-vision. The name is important. This is a time for the writer to shift from passion-hot to critic-cold. The writer pulls back from the page, rereads what she has written, reading it multiple times, looking for a variety of things. The writer may read to assess. "What's good here that I can build on, that I can make longer? What's bad here that I can cut out or rewrite completely?"

That assessment may be informed by the writer's knowledge of the kind of thing he was trying to make. Does this start with a big bold claim? Did I give a reason? Did I then include evidence to support that reason? Is there enough evidence? Could I add more? Is the next reason in a new paragraph? The writer may imagine a stranger reading the draft and think, "What sense will a reader make of this? What questions will he have? What's unclear, confusing, missing? What still needs to be done?"

The most important reason to revise is to figure out what one wants to say. Narrative writers can ask themselves, "What is this story *really* about?" just as they ask of the stories they read during reading workshop. Opinion writers can reread all their evidence and think, "What claim is actually warranted? What does the evidence suggest?" Once a writer has decided what a draft is about, the writer revises to make that meaning more prominent. Beginning and intermediate writers do this sort of revision in a concrete way. They find their best page, star the part that is most important and think, "Can I elaborate here?" Then they add onto it. They might cut out text that doesn't push forward the meaning, or move it to another part of their writing.

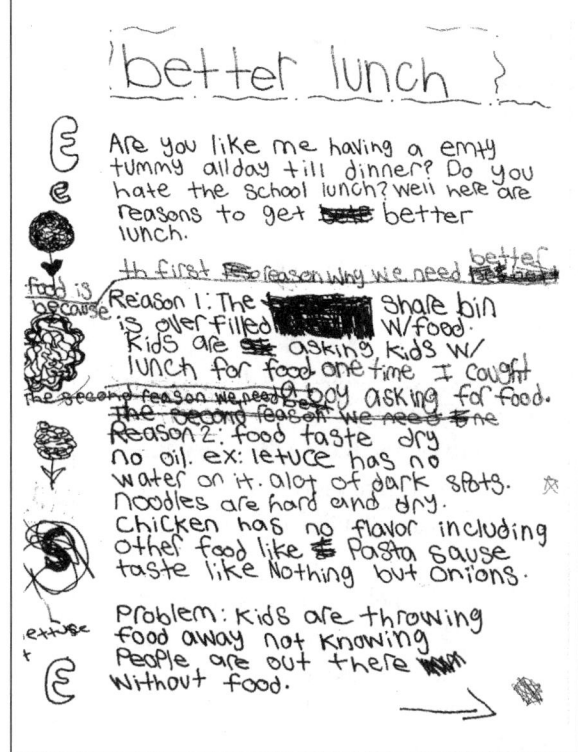

Shonda revises and makes notes for future revisions.

Revision can be akin to Batman's utility belt—there will always be something that can be done in revision to get a writer out of any jam.

Most revision work involves tackling one of three goals: structure, elaboration, or clarity. Those goals tend to be dealt with in that order. If a piece jumps all around, with no clear structure, then the writer has built a house that cannot stand. Scissors may be necessary. One page may get divided into two or three. Information may get cut up into bits and sorted into a rough filing system. "Everything about the dog's body goes here, everything about training the dog, there." A narrative might be reorganized. "The first thing that happened goes here, the next thing, there."

Once a text has structure, elaboration is usually the next consideration. Writers may learn to reread, thinking of the questions that readers would ask, then answering those questions on the page. Alternately, writers may learn to take any one part of the draft, and rewrite it more "bit by bit." A teacher might say, "It is like you took giant steps through that time. Try retelling it to me, only in baby steps. Not 'I went to the airport' but 'I picked up my suitcase and walked toward the door. Then I . . . what?'" The invitation to elaborate may sound like this: "You have written all about this in sentences of ideas. One sentence about this, one sentence about that. You are ready now to go back and write about those same things, this time writing with paragraphs, not sentences, about each of those things."

Editing. Finally, writers focus on clarity, and that focus quickly merges with the next phase of the writing process: editing. Writers read their own draft aloud, listening for places where they stumble, and those become places to clarify, to edit. Writers read, looking for places where readers will go "Huh?" or "What?" and those become places to edit.

Editing also involves fixing up. Writers check their spelling—and the most important work is not making sure that every spelling is correct so much as noticing whether a spelling seems right or wrong. Sometimes well-intended teachers think they are helping by going through a child's draft, marking every word that is wrong, leaving the child to research the correct spelling for those errors. The truth is, though, that in life one of the most important editing jobs a writer has is determining whether a word is correctly spelled or not. That's a key skill, and you need to leave that work to writers.

Many teachers ask students to rewrite words they believe are misspelled a few times in the margin, trying to get them right. Students are encouraged to mark the parts of those attempts that seem right, as well as the parts that seem off. You may want writers to take the next step and look the word up in a dictionary or, if technology is available, to use spell-check.

A few pointers about editing. First, the principles that inform the rest of your teaching also need to inform your work with editing. Presumably, when teaching novices anything—tennis, or swimming, or teaching—you do not expect mastery. By definition, a novice is someone for whom perfection is not the goal. The goal is progress. Dramatic progress, even.

The only way you can hold a novice or intermediate writer to the goal of perfection in spelling and grammar is to do that person's spelling and grammar work for him, for her, but doing so would destroy the more important and realistic goal for that writer, which is progress. So when teaching novice or intermediate writers, decide on next editing steps for them, and teach in ways that help them take those next steps themselves. Expect approximation, and celebrate progress. If a writer who hasn't done so before includes end punctuation in a draft that also includes a few fragments and run-on sentences, send up the fireworks! Celebrate that this writer has done something terrific. "Look at all those periods! Capitals too. This draft is so much easier to read."

Second, in general, an informing principle of editing is this. What you teach first during editing should later move forward and become part of drafting. If in the beginning, your kids write without paragraphs, you'll teach them to reread, cutting their page up into chunks that they tape onto their paper as paragraphs. (These won't be perfect—remember this is about approximation.) Having done that work through editing/revision, when those writers go to work on their next draft, you will want to remind them to write that draft in paragraphs from the start.

The New and Improved Editing Checklist	
End sentences with punctuation. (! ? .)	! ? .
Begin each sentence with a capital letter.	There is a bear.
Spell using all you know about how words work.	-ing running sitting hiking
Make sure others can read your writing.	
Check for run-on sentences.	STOP!
Make sure the sentences inside a paragraph fit together.	

Your goal is for more and more of these editing concerns to reach a level of automaticity. You can support writers progressing toward automaticity only if you remember that none of us achieve mastery overnight. We need systems for reminding ourselves to do things that we can almost but not quite remember to do. Little Post-it notes that say "Don't forget to paragraph!" are helpful, as are personalized word walls that contain a reasonable number of high-frequency words.

In the Up the Ladder series, you'll see time is devoted to editing, but not much time is set aside for recopying so that writers have final pieces that are perfect. Instead, we encourage you to invite students to fancy up their revised and edited writing, perhaps by making a cover, adding an "about the author" page or a back cover blurb. This means that a student's published piece might have a revision flap sticking out of the side, an extra page taped in, and is apt to contain cross-outs. In that way, students' published pieces reflect all the work they have done as writers. Most teachers find that they want to encourage students to publish their writing quickly, in all of its roughness.

Of course, there are great reasons to want perfect publications. Those can become reading material for the class, for example. But the best way to get perfect drafts from imperfect writers is to send the writers' drafts to a "publishing center," which of course is what real writers do. You might choose to do this, perhaps by having parents or other adults work at that center to help type up students' work—but we hope that you don't postpone celebrating the ending of a unit to wait for those pieces to come back corrected, as that generally takes weeks.

If you want students to produce approximately correct final drafts, then you may decide to add a day or two to every unit so there's time for children to copy over their corrected versions of their drafts. The choice is yours, but we feel that the cost of doing this is apt to be too high. For starters, it means devoting hours and hours of your evening time to red-marking each child's page—and research is clear that kids do not learn from all that work you do for them. Children learn from hearing about how to address one or two incorrect patterns in their editing—and from repeated opportunities to correct these. If you have corrected two score of errors in a child's draft and you meet with the child to overview all those corrections, it is unlikely that this conversation will actually pay off. You might have more correct work to display, but it is not likely that the time devoted to that result will lead writers to be more conventional in their next first draft.

Also, too often, as we've seen, the result of asking students to recopy drafts with your corrections is that all the energy and momentum leaves a classroom. Whereas, just the week before, writers worked with great fervor to draft, revise, and edit writing, all of a sudden that excitement is replaced with kids painstakingly recopying pages that bleed with your corrections. And too often, this stage can stretch out for many days. Our advice is—if you want kids to do this work, ask them to do it at home. Set a deadline. Don't fool yourself into thinking that this is potent teaching time—it serves a purpose, but no, it isn't your best teaching or their best learning.

Jaelynn's About the Author page

Conferring and Small-Group Work (40 minutes)

While your students work, you'll move around the classroom, trying to touch base with and respond to as many writers as possible. This is your opportunity to meet students exactly where they are at and respond accordingly. You'll see that the conferring and small-group work section could be renamed, "What Students Are Apt to Be Doing, and How You Can Respond." As you move among your students, you'll give feedback, name next steps, and help them maintain energy and momentum for writing. Donald Murray, Pulitzer Prize–winning writer, said, "The cardinal rule in a writing conference is that the writer leaves, wanting to write. The writer's energy for writing should go up, not down."

Conferring

In the beginning of your first unit, you'll just focus on getting to as many writers as possible, through a combination of quick check-ins with individuals and voiceovers to the whole class. Your goal at first will simply be to keep everyone going and on track. You will feel a bit as if you are wearing roller skates as you move around the classroom, back and forth, crouching next to writers. You'll point to something one writer has done, and give a specific compliment: "You have added dialogue that makes your characters come to life. I can almost hear them talking to me. Your dialogue helps me feel like I am in your story! Will you make sure you have added dialogue in any spot in your story where characters might be talking? Great! Back to writing!" Then you might spread this tip to the table full of children working alongside that writer: "I hope all of you have added dialogue in ways that bring your characters to life."

For another writer, you might crouch down and read part of his work out loud, reading it as if it is gold, helping the writer see the beauty and preciousness in it. "Keep going," you'll say. Your goal is to keep all of your writers writing up a storm.

To have time for these conferences (and for more fully developed ones, once kids are working with more independence), you'll want to teach your kids to self-manage. For example, if children come to you with endless little questions ("Can I get another sheet of paper? Can I sharpen my pencil?") or with constant need for reinforcement ("I wrote that ending. Will you check it?"), be sure that you respond in ways that support independence. "You are the author. What do *you* think you should do next? Good going—and next time, you don't need to come to me."

To learn to confer well with writers, it will help if you watch a few video clips of effective conferences. I'm going to channel you to two conferences—one that I lead with a fifth-grader and one that my colleague Amanda Hartman leads with a young writer. If you watch these, focus especially on the tone, the posture, the relationship that characterizes a conference. These are side-by-side conversations, with the writer, not the teacher, holding the paper and making many of the decisions. Think about the conversation you might wish your principal would have with you after watching you teach. My hunch is you'd want her to ask, "What have you been working on in your teaching?" and "How do you think it went today?" and "What next steps do you think would help you get even better as a teacher?" and that the ensuing conversation would respond to your own intentions, self-assessments, hopes.

Video: Conference with fifth-grader

Video: Amanda's conference with a young writer

You may find that your conferences don't go perfectly at first, partly because your *kids* need to learn their roles in a conference. If you ask one of your kids, "What are you working on as a writer?", that youngster may look at you like your head is screwed on wrong and say, "My book," or "My story," or "The mall" (referencing the child's topic). You'll need to teach kids that when you ask, "What are you working on as a writer?" you are asking for them to tell you what part of the writing process they have been working on and what strategies they have been using. What bullet points from the anchor chart best describes their work?

As kids talk to you about what they have been doing, they will tend to throw terms around, often talking the talk without necessarily walking the walk. One might say, "I've been elaborating with details," which sounds terrific, but be sure you follow up by asking the writer to show you where he or she has done that. You'll often find that the writer's attempts are fairly approximate, which is terrific: you have something to teach!

As a writer tells you about his or her writing work, you'll skim over the child's writing. It usually helps to look not just at that day's writing, but at the progression across days. As you look, try to think about the one most important way you could intervene to lift the level of the writer's work, not just today but in the future.

Usually in a conference, you will compliment the important breakthroughs you see the writer has made, the risks the writer has taken, or the progress he or she has made, reminding the writer to continue doing that new and important work always, on future pieces as well. Then you'll teach, aiming to teach in a way that gives the writer a big and lasting goal to work on, and that will help not only this piece but future pieces as well.

Conferring well is not easy. Most of us work a lifetime on this, and there are a few things you can do to avoid predictable problems:

Some Tips When Conferring

- Invite the writer's input before looking at his or her draft for your direction. The writer can teach you something valuable.
- Aim to teach toward a larger goal, one that writers can work toward, not only in many places of this draft, but also in future pieces of writing. (Skip teaching a small point—the first concrete thing you would change if you were the writer, such as a simile, a sound effect.)
- Expect to return many times to whatever you teach in a conference. Most writers have a few big concerns they work on across pieces, across genres. Is this a writer who needs help with structure? With elaboration? Any goal worth tackling is worth staying with across time.
- Keep realistic expectations about a writer and a piece of writing. Channel the writer toward important work that will have great payoffs, but remember that he or she can only progress step by step. A writer who is working at the second-grade level won't produce fifth-grade-level work after one conference.
- Expect your conferences to vary in length. One longer conference can set the stage for several much quicker ones.

Small Groups

If you worry about what your other students are doing while you confer, your concern is a good one. In part, the answer is that you need to alternate between conferences and small-group work, because the latter allows you to reach more students. You can anticipate and plan for predictable small groups without doing formal assessments—you can check over your writers' shoulders or listen in as they talk about their writing to quickly decide who to scoop up and gather for a small group. Also, oftentimes you can predict some of the teaching that kids will need after you have taught a minilesson.

For example, you won't need a great deal of listening and checking in to know that when you teach kids to write persuasive speeches and you ask them to gather reasons and examples for their claim, many of them will struggle with the hierarchies you are suggesting between reasons (larger umbrella categories) and supportive examples/evidence. In fact, it is more than likely that when asked to give overarching reasons, students will instead give detailed examples. So, students will write something like "We need more equipment on the playground because then we can all have more fun and because the green soccer ball is not bouncy enough." You'll want to help them realize that "then we can all have more fun" works as an overarching reason, but it'd be better for their second reason to be "and we won't have to play with old or broken equipment," with the green soccer ball functioning as one supportive example among several.

Because it is predictable that kids will need some close-in support with this complicated work, you'll probably want to lead small groups on the hierarchy involved in claims, reasons, and examples. You'll enter the day's workshop, then, knowing that kids may have this (or another) common need, and by quickly checking their work, you'll see who would most benefit from a small group addressing this.

Once you've determined the kind of work you'll support a group of kids in doing, you will want to have in mind a plan for how your group might go. You can use the small groups we describe in both the Up the Ladder series and the Units of Study as models for how to help your own kids. While sometimes it will be enough to gather kids once, for the most part, you'll want to check in on this same group of kids a few days later, for a follow-up group.

To begin any of your small groups, you'll gather a group of four or six writers (usually an even number helps) who need the same teaching, get them to huddle around you, and model something or give them a tip. In the example above, you could perhaps ask kids to all work together differentiating reasons and examples for the class essay on the need for new equipment. Perhaps you distribute a page to each of the three pairs of writers, asking

Key Features of Small Group Instruction

1. Engagement is high!

2. They are brief.

3. They are heavy with kid work and low on adult talk.

4. The kids move, the work sticks!

Responsive Small Group Coaching Tips

Choose what and how to teach.

Keep your teaching short. Read Aloud!

Use familiar texts when demonstrating.

Effectively demonstrate - name the teaching point, enact it, and name what they've seen.

Coach kids in their work.

Make an appointment to check in and follow up. ★ meet again on 2/26 each pair to read through the examples on the page, asking themselves, "Is this a reason or an example?" The page might contain sentences like these: "We need more equipment so we can play a wider variety of things." "We need more equipment because I don't like to hula hoop." As kids discussed whether each of these was a reason or an example, working in pairs, you could watch and coach lightly, moving among them as if you are the big hand on the clock and they are the digits. Then you could ask them to get out their own writing and to look at the places where they have written reasons, and working with a partner, decide if all of those reasons actually *are* reasons, or if some are examples instead. Again, after a minute of instruction, you'll channel them to dive into that work, and you meanwhile will either watch and coach or go off to other kids in the class, returning after a few minutes. That is, during a small group, the kids are doing the work.

To watch a small group in action, visit the Teachers College Reading and Writing Project website, readingandwritingproject.org, and view the video "Amanda small group on information writing" under the "Resources/Videos to Support Units of Study Implementation/Units of Study Classroom Videos/Informative/ Explanatory Writing" headings. In this small group on information writing, notice how the teacher leading that group, Amanda, gets the group started working and then coaches each writer individually. For more information about conferences and small-group work, see the chapter titled "Differentiated Feedback: Conferring with Individuals and Small Groups" in *A Guide to the Writing Workshop*.

The Mid-Workshop Teaching (approximately 3–5 minutes)

During the middle of work time, you will often want to offer your students a reminder or quick tip. You might ask writers to pause in their work and to do something particular for a few minutes. We refer to the whole-class teaching that you do in the midst of a writing workshop as "mid-workshop teaching."

To pull this off, we encourage you to stand in the middle of the classroom, and to ask for writers' attention. In a bold, clear voice, say something like, "Writers, eyes up here." The important thing is that afterward, you are quiet and give the classroom a 360-degree scan. Wait until everyone settles down, and everyone is looking at you. Then you give your mid-workshop teaching point.

Usually this is in response to what your students are—and are not—doing. For example: "Writers, I love that you are writing up a storm, but let me remind you not to get so intent on writing more, more, more that you forget to paragraph! Right now, check if you have a page that is missing paragraphs, and if so, add tildes where paragraphs belong. Then get back to your work—and remember to paragraph!"

Although the Up the Ladder sessions each contain a mid-workshop teaching point, many of these are not strictly necessary. More important is that you notice what your particular class of kids needs and use what you see to inform the mid-workshop teaching points you give. For example, if your kids are starting lots of pieces and finishing none, now is your chance to remind them to complete their writing—even if that means looking back at incomplete drafts and writing endings for several drafts. If kids are writing slowly, as if they are inscribing in marble, during a mid-workshop teaching point, you can remind them that they have just fifteen minutes left, that before the day is over their entire book needs to be done, so they need to write up a storm. If your students are growing restless and you wonder whether they can sustain writing any longer, a mid-workshop teaching point that channels students to talk for a bit can revive their energy for writing. If students are revising by adding text to the bottoms of their pages and that text only makes sense if it is integrated into the middle of their text, you can remind them to use codes or arrows or scissors to insert the new text where it belongs.

The Share (3–5 minutes)

At the end of each workshop, you'll create a way to capture the power of that day's work, to remind writers of what they have learned and to give them the satisfaction of an audience. Share sessions are both instructional and inspirational. There are half a dozen or so favorite ways to bring closure to a writing workshop, and you'll see those ways of sharing repeat often in this series. For example, often you will say to writers, "Spread your work out at your writing spot, leaving a Post-it beside the work you are most proud of." Once students have done that, you'll say something like, "Writers, for the next few minutes, we will have a silent gallery walk. During that time, read each other's writing, admiring your friends' revisions. Leave appreciative stars and smiley faces and notes beside their writing. As you do this, collect ideas for the story you might write next. Put those ideas on the Post-it you'll carry with you. Get started!"

Alternatively, you might say, "Writers, it's time to gather for a symphony share. You remember how these go. I'll act as conductor and when I point at you, you'll share out something special you wrote today. Quickly, look across your writing. Once you've found a part you are particularly proud of, get ready to share it with a partner first. Take turns rehearsing the part you select. Then we'll have our symphony."

Notice that in neither of these examples do the writers convene in the meeting area for a share session. That does happen from time to time, but it is more likely that writers are sharing with a partner or with the others at their table, and that your input is delivered from some central position in the midst of the space.

Oftentimes you will use the shares as a time for not only sharing but also for instruction. For example, one share in the Up the Ladder books begins with you saying, "Have you thought about tables of contents as something you write at the start of a whole book? Now, I want you to think of a table of contents as something you write for a single chapter. You won't actually write a TOC for each chapter. But here is the important thing—you should write each chapter so that you *could* make a table of contents for it. Organizing and categorizing are just as important *within* a chapter as they are across a whole book."

"If your chapter is like jumbled laundry, then use scissors or arrows to sort the subtopics. If you haven't written enough to sort—use this time to write super-fast. Remember, though, when you start writing, to start a new paragraph each time you begin a new subtopic."

Sometimes, the instruction comes in the form of a simple tip that reinforces earlier instruction: "Writers, voice is everything in good persuasive writing and you gotta use your voice in a way that brings your reader along to believe as you do. Right now, share your speeches with each other and make sure you have really tried to use the right words to get the audience to come along with you, to believe in the change you are proposing. If you see places where you can strengthen your writing, mark those places."

Sometimes, a share becomes a way to set students up for work to come: "Writers, tomorrow you are going to choose one entry, one story, and you'll work on it to make it into a publishable book. Before you choose, you want to make sure you have a *lot* of great entries in your notebook. So instead of spending the last five minutes of today sharing your writing, I'm going to suggest you spend the last five minutes writing one new story."

PROVISIONING YOUR WRITING WORKSHOP

Your writers don't need much to be successful within the Up the Ladder units, or frankly, within any units. There are no special classroom arrangements needed or elaborate lists of materials that will keep you running from store to store. However, you'll want to keep in mind a few critical considerations when arranging your classroom and provisioning your students.

Where will students gather during minilessons?

In most workshop classrooms, students gather together for the minilesson on a large carpet that's prominently located in a corner of the classroom. Students typically sit in assigned spots next to a long-term writing partner. Often, the carpet is framed by the classroom library. It helps if the charts that are predominant in a unit are accessible from the meeting area, so you can reference and add to as you teach. It also helps if there is a chair for you and if you have easy access to an easel and chart paper. Although it is not necessary, many teachers find it useful to have access to a document camera and projector or to other technology they can use to enlarge their own writing, mentor texts, and students' writing. It will be important for that equipment to be positioned in such a way that you needn't teach in a "stand and deliver" fashion. Many teachers position projectors so they can reach them as they sit at the front of the meeting area.

Where will students write during work time?

Most teachers assign work spots for students. This way, when the minilesson ends with the words, "Off you go," writers can quickly get to their assigned spot and begin work. Many teachers use tables or desks and also floor spots around the room as work spaces. If there are desks in the classroom, many teachers tell kids that the wells of those desks can be private, but the tops of the desks are public real estate. This means that students need not remain at their own desks throughout the day. Also, it can be helpful to position partners close to each other so they can share easily. If students are seated next to their writing partners, they can turn and talk with partner during the mid-workshop teaching point and share without a lot of commotion. Many teachers encourage partners to listen in on the conferences that they have with individuals.

How will students access the materials they need for writing?

Most teachers decide to set up a writing center in their classroom, designating one area as the spot where all the writing resources will be stored. This way, students can independently access the writing materials they need whenever they are writing, without having to raise their hand and ask for permission.

Many writing centers contain:

- Bins holding several different kinds of lined paper, some in booklets and some not
- Staplers
- Three-hole punches and brads
- Revision flaps
- Tape
- Post-it notes
- Copies of the mentor text(s)
- Dictionaries
- Books on writing well
- Dictionaries or thesauruses

How much writing paper will I need?

A lot! At the start of a unit, we recommend you make a big pile of each kind of paper you're offering to students so that students don't run out during writing time. You should expect that students will go through several booklets in a week, with some students writing even more. *It is very important for students to write on one side of the page only*, which allows them to revise their writing by cutting it apart and adding in extra half-sheets of paper.

Where will students store their writing?

We recommend you provision students with their own two-pocket folder, and that you mark one side of the folder with a green dot for writing in progress and

the other side with a red dot for finished writing. At the end of each workshop, students can quickly decide where their writing belongs and file it appropriately. Of course, just because writing is filed into the red dot side, that doesn't mean students won't revisit it. Instead, you will want to encourage students to pull their writing out of the red dot side and revise it as they learn new strategies.

In Bend III of the Narrative unit, students are introduced to writing notebooks. These are often marble composition notebooks that students personalize with favorite photos, quotes, stickers, and their own drawings. Students move between rehearsing for ideas in their notebook and drafting on loose-leaf paper, which is then stored in their writing folder. This work prepares students to use their writing notebook in any of the upper-grade Units of Study. The notebook does not play a role in other Up the Ladder units, so you may want the notebooks that students use in Bend III of the Narrative unit to be temporary, small ones.

What books will I need?

Writers read, and the reading they do nurtures their images of good writing. It is important, therefore, that you give kids access to wonderful texts that resemble those you hope they will write. A rich library is an invaluable resource for writers.

On the other hand, you needn't fret terribly over making sure that you have every title that is mentioned in the Up the Ladder books or the Units of Study in Opinion, Information, and Narrative Writing series. First, there are usually just a small number of touchstone books in a unit of study. And secondly, even those few titles are cases in point and you could theoretically substitute another book for the one we highlight.

How important are materials to the success of the writing workshop?

You'll quickly see that the writing workshop does not require a lot of materials. Contrast the teaching of writing with the teaching of reading, for example! I often say that you only need to provide your students with a pen and some paper, and you are set for a successful writing workshop.

Whereas it is true that you don't absolutely need a lot of materials to teach writing, the flip side is also true. Materials can play a vital role in the success of your writing workshop. Take them seriously.

Above all, we encourage you to study the guidance that each Up the Ladder book provides on the kinds of paper that we recommend you offer to students. One of the biggest lessons we learned from watching these units being piloted was that when kids were writing on paper that seemed "just right" for them, the paper itself seemed to exert a powerful force. Meanwhile, when kids were writing on paper that seemed either way too easy or way too overwhelming, the paper also wielded a powerful force—and not necessarily in a good way. Our suggestion, then, is to pay attention to the advice each book offers on paper. Be sure that your kids are not all writing on the same sort of paper, and be sure that the paper a child uses changes several times across the unit of study. If your students' energy for writing ever seems to plateau, consider finding a way to jazz up the paper. You'll be amazed at the difference that stickers for decorating pages can make.

It is not only important that you provide a variety of paper and give guidance over which paper seems just right for particular writers, it is also important that you give kids plenty of paper, and that you insist that they write on one side of the page only so the paper can be revised easily.

Pens are as important as paper—and yes, I encourage you to channel kids to write in pen, not pencil. Their writing is easier to see, to read, and to celebrate, when it is written in pen, and pen doesn't allow for erasures, which is an added benefit because you will want to see and to celebrate kids' rough drafts and revisions (and to steer kids away from fretting endlessly over a particular spelling during their first-draft writing). You can rally kids' enthusiasm for writing and revision by providing them with special colored pens. A purple "revision pen" can make the world of difference!

For more detailed information about preparing your classroom for effective writing workshop, please see the "Provisioning a Writing Workshop" chapter in *A Guide to the Writing Workshop*.

Chapter 3

Addressing Predictable Concerns

MY COLLEAGUES AND I have been doing this work for a while (coming up on three decades). We have helped thousands of teachers teach writing workshop and have gleaned insights from watching that work in action. We know that there will be some key concerns that tend to come up in your teaching of writing, and in this section, I'll give you my best, most high-leverage advice for addressing some of those predictable problems.

Above all, I also encourage you to join the Facebook groups for Units of Study to learn from colleagues across the globe who are ready to support you, answer questions, and share their own ideas, photos of their charts, student work, and systems of recording assessment notes. You'll find yourself in a community like no other, and you'll feel the encouragement of that community, of that I can promise you.

So now, to answering a few common questions:

What if my teaching has gotten ahead of my student's work (e.g., What if I'm teaching them to revise and they haven't finished drafting)?

There will be times when you feel as if your teaching has gotten ahead of your students. You may have taught them three ways to revise and nudged them to reread and revise both their books—meanwhile, many of them haven't finished their second book, let alone begun revising it. In those instances, there are a few things to do.

First, know that sometimes the unit is paced very quickly, and the fact that your kids need a catch-up day is a consequence of the unit itself. Often, though, the misalignment between your teaching and your kids' work should cause a bit of concern. Be self-critical. Have your minilessons lasted more than ten minutes? Are you allowing kids to interject with questions and comments that are swamping the minilessons and making them too long? Are you ad-libbing on and on, way off the transcript? Are you not giving kids a full fifty minutes (or an hour) for writing workshop? Can you find more minutes in your day? Are kids talking instead of working during writing time, or using colored pencils to turn writing time into art class? Are they dawdling, and needing more voiceovers where you say things like, "Your pencils should be flying. I want to hear the turn of the page as you go from writing one page to the next"?

All the self-assessment in the world won't change the fact that your teaching has gotten ahead of your kids, and you'll want to give them time to catch up. In this instance, many teachers decide to insert a "repertoire day." On a repertoire day, you'll remind students of all the strategies they have learned so far and help them know that it's their job to decide what work needs to be done, and to draw on their full repertoire of skills and strategies to do that work. The anchor charts in the unit are a wonderful resource to help you lead this type of lesson. You might model thinking aloud about the strategies on the anchor chart and looking at your writing to see which of these strategies you have used so far, and which you haven't. Then you might show students how you quickly jot a self-assignment for yourself ("I am going to try harder to bring my characters to life with dialogue and inner thinking"). Then you can push students to do the same work, rereading their writing with the points on the anchor chart in mind and giving themselves a self-assignment for what they will do when they leave the meeting area.

Repertoire lessons have two major goals. The first, as mentioned, is to support students in drawing on prior learning. The second is increasing agency and independence in your writers. Nothing can be more important.

What if my students' writing doesn't show that my teaching is sticking?

Imagine that you've taught your students to include a variety of information. You've taught them to paragraph. And yet, when you look at their writing, it looks like a blob of rambly ranting—information on one subtopic and another, overlapping with no paragraphs in sight. You know you have taught them to sort their information into piles, into paragraphs—but you don't see evidence that your teaching has stuck.

First, you'll want to ensure that your students were given opportunities to practice your teaching point both independently and with teacher or peer support. Then, make sure that you've given your students multiple entry points to whatever it is you've been teaching. For example, if a child's IEP suggests that this student needs organizational accommodations or the student is new to English and his current stage of language acquisition is still at the sentence-production level, you will want to be sure you have provided the child with the tools and experiences that make your expectations valid.

If your students do *not* have known obstacles, you need to let them know they are accountable for what they have been taught. You need to convey to them that you expect them to try out what they are learning. You will want to remind them of the anchor chart and even make mini-copies of this chart, showing them how to code their writing for where they have done the things on the anchor chart as a way to hold themselves accountable.

If your teaching hasn't been sticking, you'll probably want to use your mid-workshop teaching or your share to hold kids accountable. You might say, "Everyone pause right now. Let's look at the anchor chart. Note the first bullet? Point to where you have done that in your piece. If you haven't done that, fix it right now." Then again, you might ask students to mark five places in their information text where they wrote with specific information, sharing those spots with a partner. Getting students to concretely identify places where they have done the work you asked them to do can also be a way to nudge kids to get busy.

You also can also push accountability by using a mentor text, showing students how to use a mentor text as a reminder of the work they need to do. The student might look at the mentor text and think, "This text has paragraphs. Does my work have paragraphs? This text has an introduction that names the subtopics it'll cover. Maybe I should do that."

What if my students seem dutiful and compliant, rather than deeply invested?

It is impossible to underestimate the power of specific, honest compliments. Study the child's work and note something quirky, something a bit different, and note especially if the writer has done this more than once. Then call the writer's attention to it and compliment in ways that feel personal. "I just love the way you have used kid-talk here when you tell what your character was thinking. She's a kid—and you make her thoughts feel like a kid's thoughts. No one taught you to do that—you thought it up on your own and that is so like you. You are always finding ways to make things special."

While your students are working, you'll want to do what you can to encourage them to draw on all they have learned across the unit. Keep in mind that work that they do first during revision can later move forward in the process and become part of their drafting. So at first, students will revise their narratives by going back to parts that they have written, thinking, "I should act this out and then write it, bit by bit." Later, however, those same students can draft stories by envisioning the scene, almost dramatizing in their minds as they write. Similarly, when working on information writing, students will at first revise to add specifics such as numbers, colors, and quotations, and later when they draft, they'll write with that sort of concrete information from the start.

This same progression will happen with lessons that students learn about editing. For example, you'll see that early in a unit, many of your students don't paragraph. Then your instruction will accentuate the importance of paragraphing as a way to fix up a completed draft, and after a bit, you should expect to see that even first-draft writing is paragraphed from the start.

What if I have writers who don't like to revise?

Revision represents the front edge of a student's learning. This is where the new learning happens. You'll want to embrace revision, to see it as something that all good writers do, especially when a draft has potential and merits further work. Revision is not a form of correction for bad writing! Instead, it is a way to invest in writing that has real potential.

You'll probably find that it takes a bit of luring to draw your students toward revision. Know that supplying them with revision tools can make the work much more appealing. Writers of all ages seem to be very fond of writing tools, and that will certainly be the case for your youngsters. Special purple revision pens go a long way, as do scissors, flaps, large colorful Post-its, brads. Do everything you can to help your youngsters see writing as more like playing in clay than inscribing in marble. You can even create bulletin board titles—"Make It Messy to Make It Clear"—that celebrate drafts with crossed-out sections and inserts. Of course, although work that students once did during revision will move forward in the writing process and be part of an early draft, hopefully your students will continue to embrace revision as they grow as writers.

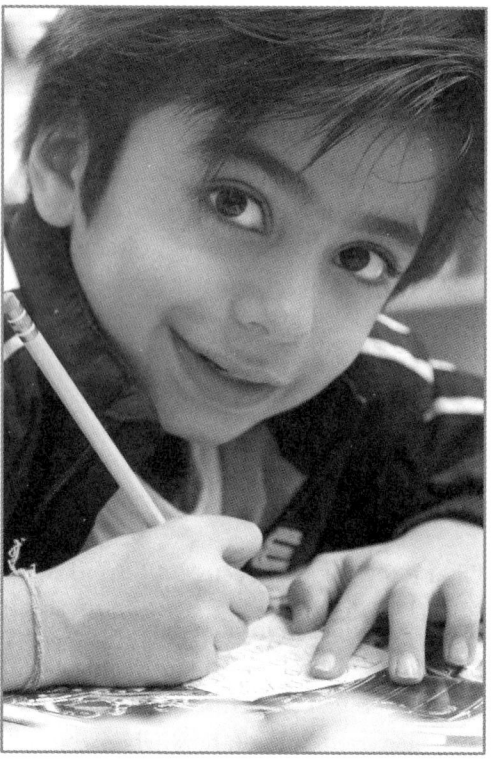

What might the long-term plan be for a school's use of Up the Ladder units? Might next year's teacher reteach one of these units?

Ideally, if students have already experienced Up the Ladder units, they are no longer novices in the genres of narrative, information, and opinion writing, and they will be ready for the grade-level Units of Study curriculum for that grade. For some classes, this may not be the case and if so, your school might decide to reteach the Up the Ladder units, echo-writing the demonstration writing and substituting new mentor texts so all the examples are new. Instead of the teacher modeling with a collection of dragon pictures, for example, that teacher might model with a collection of superhero pictures.

Then, too, a teacher may decide to teach just one bend of the Up the Ladder books as a way to warm her class up before diving into one of the original units. Before launching into the fifth-grade *The Research-Based Argument Essay* unit, a teacher might teach Bends III and IV (or just Bend IV) of the Up the Ladder Opinion unit. Before launching into fiction, a fourth- or fifth-grade teacher might teach Bend II of the Up the Ladder Narrative unit.

Then, too, these units can be given a new lease on life if they are lent to a school that visits your school, sees your students' success, and decides they want to launch the Units of Study. Your generosity can make the world of difference to a new community of teachers and students, and to the larger world.

Chapter 4

Assessment

ASSESSMENT will be infused into every day of your teaching. It isn't something that happens on specific assessment days. Every day and every minute of your time in the classroom is a moment for assessment. Writers write (or don't write), and you assess and respond.

Assessment will happen like breathing. You'll see that a child is staring up into space, not writing, and you'll pull in close to ask, "What are you thinking?" and the ensuing conversation is all about assessment. You'll see that a child has thrown tons of random facts down on a page, and that assessment will jolt you into remembering that learners need repeated reminders, and you'll say to the whole class in a voiceover, "Don't forget to paragraph. Each paragraph holds one subtopic."

The important thing to know about this every day, minute-by-minute sort of assessment is that above all, it is your teaching you are assessing. You aren't evaluating whether the child is, or is not, somehow acceptable. The progress or lack of progress that a child makes doesn't make that child acceptable. I'm reminded of a sign hanging prominently at the grocery chain, Stew Leonard's: "The customer is always right." In a sense, it is best to approach assessment during a writing workshop with that same attitude: "The learner is always right." That stance will allow you to learn how to teach from the learner. When you see the child's engagement or lack of engagement in writing, you need to think, "What is this suggesting about whether I have succeeded in recruiting this learner to invest in writing? What's next for this writer?" When you see the child's progress or lack of progress structuring his or her writing, you can think, "To what extent have I succeeded in helping this child know how and want to structure his or her draft?"

Although you will keep a close eye on the cues that can help you make constant small corrections in your teaching, you will probably also want some larger assessment to help you know whether your teaching is on course. I'm interested in my bone density, so every year I am given a bone density scan, and my results are charted alongside those of other women my age, and an expert interprets the results by comparing and contrasting my results with those of the others. These assessments influence decisions about the course of treatment.

In the teaching of writing, there is a way to conduct more formal assessments, and the good news is that it doesn't require either fancy technology or outside experts. All you need to do is to devote a day's writing workshop time to preassessment, a day's writing workshop to post-assessment, and then to study the results. For your narrative assessment, you can say to writers, "Today, write your best personal narrative. Do this all on your own, without help from me. You can plan your story, draft it, and if you want, you can revise it, but the story must be done in fifty minutes. Go!" You can give similar directions for an information text and for opinion writing. Give the same directions on a day prior to your unit and a day right after the unit.

You might be surprised that I'm not suggesting you give the whole class a prompt so as to more easily compare what they do—and, of course you can decide to do that if you wish. I think you'll see that it an illusion, however, that

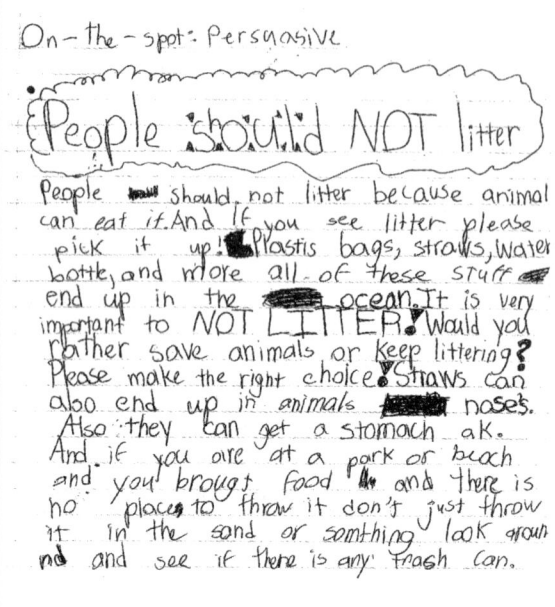

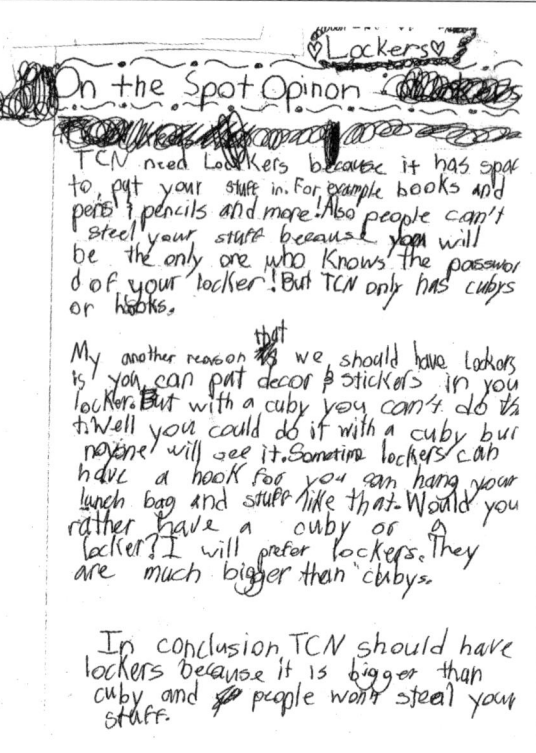

Marisa's Opinion Writing Pre-On-Demand *(left)* and Post-On-Demand *(right)*

a shared prompt or common topic gives everyone an equal starting line. Here is an example of one child's opinion writing prior to and just after the Up the Ladder Opinion unit. People write more or less well depending on their relationship to a topic, and there is no topic that will be equally relevant to all writers. Therefore the easiest way to give every writer an even playing field is to allow them to decide on the topics they'll write about. "Write a story about something that happened to you once." "Write a book about a topic you know well, a topic you could teach to other kids." "Write an opinion about something you think should be changed in the world."

You may want to remind the writers of what constitutes a good narrative, a good information text, a good opinion piece—or not. In the end, writers need to know how to write without a checklist guiding them. If you want to say, "Here is a checklist that tells you what constitutes an effective story/information text/opinion piece," you can use the ones that are in the Up the Ladder books, which can easily be found in the online resources.

The important thing is that whatever the conditions are for the first on-demand, you replicate them exactly at the end of the unit when you conduct a second on-demand writing assessment. And then, you look between what the writer was able to make prior to your teaching, and what the writer has produced after your teaching, and there, before you, are the data you need to assess your teaching—and our shared curriculum.

In the Units of Study kits, the book *Writing Pathways* formalizes this, and includes rubrics and benchmark texts there to help you gauge your writers' progress. Just bear in mind when you look at those texts, that the levels we set there are aligned to the Common Core State Standards, which are extraordinarily ambitious standards. In the end, there is no "Arbitrator on High" who can say what levels of achievement are and are not realistic for all kids to achieve by this or that grade. And in any case, even if there are agreed-upon standards for what kids should be able to know and do, the conversation then must turn to who—or what—is being evaluated when kids do or do not reach those standards. After all, in the end, it is on us to take kids the distance.

It is on us, the nation, to provide kids with teachers who have time to study and to plan. In Finland, teachers have three times as much planning time as do teachers in the United States. It is on us, the nation, to provide kids with the access to children's literature that will help them want to write, and that will help them have the richest possible language in their bones. It is on us, the nation, to protect our system of public education for those who look at students and see dollar signs. It is on us, the nation, to be sure that all kids come to school, feeling safe enough to be able to focus on learning. It is on us, the nation, to be sure that all kids know their lives, their ideas, their opinions are worth putting on the page, and to know that people will listen with rapt attention.

Children's progress as writers can be dramatic, and we can take great satisfaction in that progress. In the end, assessment leads to reflection, to taking stock, and that work leads to activism.